# take a stroll with me

a collection of poetry by mallory shoemaker

First paperback edition, June 2025.

*Cover art by Morgan Elliott (@thewildpeachstudio)*
*Interior design by Sarah Goldschadt (sah-rah.com)*

ISBN: 979-8-9892376-2-3 (Hardcover)
ISBN: 979-8-9892376-5-4 (Paperback)
ISBN: 979-8-9892376-6-1 (Audiobook)
ISBN: 979-8-9892376-3-0 (Ebook)
Library of Congress Control Number: 2024900915

Published by: malarayofsunshine / Mallory Shoemaker
PO Box 15, Milton, WA 98354

For rights, permissions, or appearances please contact:
mallory@malarayofsunshine.com

*To all the people who broke me,*
*led me, and loved me into my now—thank you.*

*"I'll never again speak to many*
*of the people who loved me into this moment,*
*just as you will never speak*
*to many of the people who loved you into your now.*
*So we raise a glass to them—and hope that*
*perhaps somewhere, they are raising a glass to us."*
—John Green, *The Anthropocene Reviewed*

## table of contents

## *social quips*

shiny lips,
social quips
never do me right.
ruffled sheets
and limousines
fall into my sight.
hold me
close and
let me stay,
'twined around your
toes.
where you start
and where i
stop,
what a grand unknown.
ruffled sheets,
abandoned clothes,
scattered on the
rug.

take a stroll with me

## speed of light

everything crawling at the speed of light.
it looks like it's day, but it's really night.
everything is dark, but it's really light.
tell me, when do opposites attract?

## *shh, don't cry*

and once again i'm at a loss for words,
there's nothing left to say when everything is known.
 it's hard to make things new,

when everything gets older.
shh, don't cry.
shh, don't yell.
it'll all get better soon, you'll see.
the world doesn't always kiss and tell.

so someday you'll see.
we'll find a way.
but for tonight?
shh, don't cry.
let me hold you
tightly.

# airlines and postcards

send me a postcard over seas,
through the airlines,
from you to me.

where are you,
when you write?
pretend you're here with me tonight.

don't tell me what i want to hear,
tell me what you want to say.
that may make it seem okay.

still,
i close my eyes and wish it all back,
to how it was.
you don't remember,

i know.

i read your postcard,
it broke my thoughts.

my heart spilled.
soft, onto the paper.
gentle,

return to sender.

## business bears

teddy bears and i in a business-like group meeting,
talking about popping corn and how long it requires heating.
soon as my hair falls out of curls they seem to stop eating,
it's then i slowly realize that i've somehow stopped believing. ◇◇

## *gentleman caller*

gentleman caller:
i do not understand why,
if when absence makes the heart grow forder,
all you do is cry.
i may never be decided, or turn over my hand.
so i'm sorry dearest sir,
you'll have to make another plan.

# *take a stroll with me*

"take a stroll with me," said the stardust to the moon, ☾
"we'll talk and see and touch and taste what may be over soon.

when then the sun has gone to bed and the sky remains alone,
that's when i'll take you to the beach and we'll each find a soft sandstone.

on those stones of sand we'll etch—our names—and take them each in hand,
then with a wish a kiss a swish we'll throw them off the land.

and though the sea will eat them whole and gently they will sink,
our love will be remembered more permanent than ink."

# *the world is my canvas*

the world is my canvas,
and every thought a wish.
inside my head the words are met,
by black and blue and red.
so take my hand and let us go,
beyond the sunset, green.
into the dreams of wishing rocks,
into the great beyond.

 *buzzless bees*

winter nights, summer kites, windblown hair;
rolling hills and captains' wills followed through with care.
all the wingless hummingbirds, all the buzzless bees;
lonely howls, balding owls, separated "we."

## haplessness of wishing wells

the haplessness of wishing wells,
erotic depth a plight;
dancing mice and wedding bells—
may vanish in the night.
whisper softly in my ear what
you wish be your delight,
when closer i soon then become—
i'll make your feelings bright. ✧

## toppum hat

welcome sir, your toppum hat
is sitting blank upon your head.
did you know there's one of that
and of that one it's nigh to dead.

# *hollow in the morning*

hollow in the
morning,
hollow in the
night;
taking home no diamond
ring,
but dancing with the
king.

## this empty way

this empty way,
this open heart;
the way it ends,
the way it starts.
a lullaby of eerie style,
sinks down
and down
and on
for miles.

take a stroll with me

# gunmetal grey

gunmetal
grey,
what did you say?
underground
way,
where do you stay?
flowers in
may,
all fun and play.

## *les miserable*

les miserable,
oh, frightful day.
and in the fog,
hope disarray.
it gently moved,
then slipped away—
that cold 'n dreary,
frightful day.

## hopeful, hopeful firefly

sunshine of my heart;
come back, come out to play.
happiness of grey—
spilled open to impart.

at long last, welcome back, dear muse;
my most welcomed inspiration—
the wondrousness causation,
my joy in all dear hues.

be charming in the moment,
be daring in descent.
sweet love, so strong and potent—
with thoughts anew, unspent.

let joy and laughter fill your cup—
when offered in atonement.
twas when the shapeless tree was bent,
then warm came bubbling up.

gentle, gentle butterfly,
in the case of hope amend.
hopeful, hopeful firefly—
my good and dearest friend.

## *i like*

white things and blue things,
and old things and new things.
lace things and plaid things,
happy things, not sad things.

# nightlife ♪ ♪

i do believe in fairies,
and dance the night away.
we fly and chase the raindrop dew,
until the break of day.

when the moon is high and lit,
the nightlife comes alive.
be careful where you step, my pet,
for jesters gone awry.

the queen on heightened glory soars,
'fore iridescent eyes.
her praises ring melodious charms,
from gentlemen in ties.

the courtiers' prancing waltz
erupts in trumpet cries,
children gulp down chocolate malts,
and want no beddy-byes.

and so begins a fairy scene
as from the days of old,
when children were entranced by such,
and the stories were retold.

when next you see a gleam
of diamond in the brush,
know delight of fae and queen,
is whispered with a "hush!" ～～

## *young sailors* ～～

blow in, bright breeze from shores afar
and tell of where the young sailors are
for whence they went they have not come
and rough, the sea is mute and dumb

the stars dip down and touch the waves
and echo their reflection, grave
in their faces does reflect
this new, new world and it's defect

when morning dawns and breaks the day
the caves have nothing more to say
for our good luck of treasured gold
the men before have sold their souls

# a close distance

the distance of a comfort
is not not far away
hold my hand tonight

## *come with me*

come with me
down
    to
      the
        sea
and where we were
we'll
    never
      be
        again
into the foam i'll race you
(but only if you want to)

take a stroll with me

## *when the world is on your doorstep*

when the world is on your doorstep
don't let yourself be alone
let the wind carry hope to your lips
the breeze of soft imagining

be real and live in truest form
vivid colours in your mind
act like keys to roads unknown
beginning new adventures

ocean waves and seashell caves
names made out of echoes
seahorses are the butterflies
in the view made out of bubbles

## the silent snow

the silence of the snow falls softly
subduing the thoughts
that tumble in my head

i hear echoes of the wishes
my heart and my head
battle to rationalize

only for a moment as
the sky lets itself fall apart
everything is quiet

the moments pass more quickly
and when i blink i know
the illusion i cling to will vanish

the world will be covered
and i won't remember
anymore • • •

## the bend

begin at the beginning
and talk me to the end
my mistress my demise
is coming 'round the bend
her waist so lean and proper
her head held high with grace
it's ironically befitting
that i cannot see her face.

## *unheard smells*

taste the feeling
let it go
ever onwards,
forward.
breathe in every
unheard smell,
upside down and,
backwards.

take a stroll with me

## ruffled feathers

ruffled feathers lift me up
blue sky catches my hair
breathe in the atmosphere
gradual, time passes
i forget my lungs
breathing seems
unreal
. . . . . .

## *wanting*

wanting, not just for the sake of wanting,
not knowing how to be awake.
whispered wishes and unknown hearts,
wants and needs slowly drift apart.
open my mouth as if to speak,
only air comes out.
i hear far off voices call my name,
empty rain rolls down the drain.
the feelings of sleep elude me,
my wandering heart embarks.
i've almost become a skeleton,
with dreams of life forgotten.
write down who i was for me,
tell people of those moments.
if only, if only tomorrow reset,
the way it began and the things i regret.
when you wanted something,
and i wanted less.

## chandelier

windows open, breeze or not
the summer tries to stream in, hot.
i hear crickets loudly trill,
as the atmosphere falls still.

the moon and sun say day is done,
and switch for evening places.
the stars that follow simply come,
with bright and shining faces.

looking up the chandelier
of light and fractured mirrors,
reflected from the nighttime sky,
the twinkle of a lover's eye.

## royal, flushed

after all
i still believe—
our hearts are open,
free to float.
the flower's call
attracts the bees—
their arms are open,
royal, flushed.
the sunshine's hours
golden gleam—
the moment's open,
free to hope.
summer spirits,
heat and mirth—
our eyes are open,
eager, rushed.

## yesterday's plan

forgiveness is the beginning of the end
it's how we break and how we mend
from moments to daydreams
and back again—
tomorrow's an echo of yesterday's plan

*warm tea in autumn*

clear my senses
welcome in the outside air
drinking drains my cup

take a stroll with me

## *wrap me up*

wrap me up
in your eyes
underneath the moonless sky
hopeful you could
understand
without me saying why

## inside song

read to me from your
thoughts among the stars
open your heart and play me
the song you keep inside
venture on, the daylight breaks,
into a most peculiar dawn
see my breath call out your name
and whisper clouds again

take a stroll with me

## *(two-three) waterfalls*

every
waterfall
began
underground,
between
avalanche
sneezes
and
overwhelmed
geodes

## *friendly shadow*

✦ i wish i may with all my might
　follow the star i see tonight

　　where up it hangs and glows to guide,
　　to there i'll leap and learn to fly.
　　　　〜〜

　　come fae, come child, come one and all
　　to hear the forest's law;

　　the one who reigns and rules it all
　　is coming from afar!

　　a spark of light brings much delight,
　　as ribbons of my hopes ignite—

　　and through it all a laugh rings out
　　soon followed by a shout,

　　the night's alive with happy things,
　　and magic bounds about. ✧

　　of golden spells and mermaid bells,
　　the twinkling stars do arc,

　　drawing pictures painted, bright
　　of paths marked at the start.

　　find ye near here don't turn away,
　　though closer than you ought;

　　for if you listen carefully
　　you'll hear the evening's plot:

　　as up he rises, quite a sight,
　　mischievous his game

the shadows scatter in his wake,
for fear of being tamed.

too soon i see the moonlight smile
as it begins to fade,

the darkness bleeds into the light
and to the sky i'm bade.

the clouds part sides like ocean waves
and i am marked as nave,

torn from this place of quiet hope,
and from the boy it gave.

through listless nights to bring him back,
in all my dreams the strength i lack.

though separated from his gaze
my memory aches to keep him brave

so with chin held high though spirits low,
i gently sing a soft echo;

the what, the when, the how, the why
are nowhere near the way to fly

if i knew then what i know now,
i'd learn to leave and let it go.

into the dull and empty sky
i finally break and start to cry,
for shadows found and lost.

## *the key*

the setting sun could not
open her
the rising moon was the key

take a stroll with me

## *corners of the earth*

a drop of rain was
not enough
to quench her thirst
for she had not yet been
to the
corners of the earth

# ☾ *picture of the moon*

i took a picture of the moon
and put it in my pocket
moondust fell behind me
with every step i took

take a stroll with me

## warm gift

bold;
the sun shines down
warming the earth.
and the ground
brave and true,
soaks up the gift
to carry into the night

## between laughter

there is something strange
about waiting for the silence
between laughter—
as though everyone is in on it
and when the next wave comes
we are delighted by the sound,
a rapture somehow unexpected.

## a deal

i made a deal with the devil.
not for beauty,
♡ not for love,
but for time.
for more places traveled,
people met,
self discovered.
i sold my soul to the devil
and the devil was <u>me.</u>

## *mirrors distort*

we are so quick to reject
our reflection in the mirror
when it is different than yesterday.
always forgetting that mirrors distort...
the journey we took,
the people we've come from,
and the places we've left behind.

take a stroll with me

## camping at nighttime

hot and cold
bodies under blankets, feet out.
no lights, but moonlight- crickets.
stars so bright they shine even when eyes are closed.
deep breaths of all things being possible.

## *kindness, rooted*

your kindness crept in through the tips of my toes
and didn't stop 'til it had reached my nose.
when i felt the tickle start to rise,
i smiled, quick, and closed my eyes.
a single tear rolled down my cheek.
your kindness, it had rooted deep
and made my soft eyes start to leak.

## *there is no map*

there is no map
to lead us as we walk,
we must follow
the sun in our eyes,
the wind in our ears,
and the hope in our hearts.

## *you can heal now*

dig in
scrunch your toes into the earth
you can heal now
no one is measuring your worth
by the things you do
or the people you know
take a deep breath
and just
*let go* ~~~~~~

## *organs*

no one warns you that your heart and lungs
are not different organs.
so now here i am,
trying to remind my heart how to breathe.

## *unnerving*

when you know which way to go, a sign is reassuring, ⟶
but when you're searching, far from home, a sign is more unnerving.

take a stroll with me

# *without you*

peace comes in the stillness,
in the subtle, little ways.
calm comes when i'm breathing
and quiet lifts the haze.

at night my heart betrays my brain
and i, the hopeless mediator,
attempt to listen yet again
as they start the story over.

all the words you didn't say
that somehow i still heard—
felt like hopeful subtext,
that i used to build our world.

sleep comes slowly now you're gone,
so aware of hours passing.
the space you used to fill feels wrong,
i leave it hollow, asking.

in the dark i miss you most,
but daylight makes me stronger.
maybe i'll be better soon;
i'll try a little longer.

## a selfish shot

this should have killed me.
the bullet shot right through.
the coldness of your words
like you knew just which to use.
i know you aren't malicious,
that you didn't shoot to kill.
fear got the better of you,
and you took aim without skill.
i don't blame you for my heartache
as i lay here on the ground.
you did just what you had to,
to keep yourself around.

take a stroll with me

# *jazz*

i fill the room with jazz
hoping it will fill me, too.
no music quite understands
the hollow of a body
that holds a broken heart
like the melancholy trumpets
and all the other parts
of *jazz*.

## perspective equals view

i don't think in absolutes
of if it's "black" or "white."
humans live more spastically ~~~
we make up "wrong" or "right."
the devil is in the details
and maybe god is, too.
i refuse to force an outcome,
perspective equals view.

## my worst mistake

sometimes i feel like bursting with everything i hold.
authentically i live my truths- wild, raw, and bold.
if, at the end, my worst mistake
was a lack of being cold
i'll remember that, when i am old;
i lived a life i chose.

## *when i am done*

you broke me
and you do not get to witness
the slow and steady pace
at which i put myself back together
when i am done
rising from this pain
my transformation will be complete
and you will sit in ash

## *heart trust*

thinking about speaking
keeps the words inside
i realize how important
it is to see your eyes
when i do, it feels like trust
a place i can be seen
even if they are not said,
you know the words between
the morning after breaking
i feel brand new again
you hold my heart
inside your chest
as effortless as breathing

## october flirts with me

october flirts with me
she holds her hands to window panes
and sets young trees aflame.
i smell her in the piney air
and see her through the veil—
of fog and mist that's hanging low
and clouds that threaten early snow. ✗
her body sways among the branches
of barren trees caught up in dances.
on mountain tops with frosty tips
and shortened days between her lips—
october flirts with me.

take a stroll with me

## *the most powerful magic*

life is beautiful and messy and every day i fall more in love with the world and everyone in it. it makes me feel full and empty and little pieces of me chip off on every person i bump up against, but pieces of them chip off on me, too and i am a selfish collector of these things that make us happy and sad and everything in between. i'll crack myself open and pour myself out so you can cross the street without soiling your shoes and all i ask is that you tell me a story; a story about the last time you felt so alive that you wanted to scream or the last time you felt so loved that you thought you'd never wonder what love is or feels like again. other people don't break our hearts, we do– by being so open that people can walk in with their shoes on and use their inside voices and knock over our favorite vases, but don't close the door because then the friend who will hold your hand and drive you to the doctor even though you're much too old can't come in and the flowers from your neighbor's yard will never be offered across the fence and you might not ever learn how to make tamales. so buy lemonade from every kids' stand you walk past, carry an emergency twenty (even if it isn't for your own emergency), and give out smiles like little offerings of hope — because you never know who is in a moon phase of their life and your kindness may be the only sunshine they can store up to get themselves through the long night ahead. so every day when i go out i look for the worms on my path and move them back to dirt because i've been a worm and all i wanted was someone to put me back in the dirt. they will tell you that hearts are not meant to be worn on sleeves, but i think they are wrong—hearts are meant to held in outstretched hands and passed and shared so we can feel the weight of one another's humanity and try to wrap our arms around it and pull it close and collectively heal. yesterday is forever a part of us and tomorrow is never guaranteed and today is the only "me" and "we" that we can ever truly know. so let's do our best and be generous with grace and never wonder what love is again because love is the most powerful magic of all and the more we give away the more comes back to us.

## *i will bloom*

you waited for me
and did not rush me
or push me
or leave me
and i will bloom
under your watchful eye
listening to me say, "i'm not ready yet"
day after day
until one day
because you were soft,
because you were gentle,
because you were kind—
i will bloom
and you will be there to see me
and celebrate me
and together we will bask in the sun.

# thank you

To my wonderful family: mum, Kimmi, and Becca—thank you for being my constant cheerleaders in every crazy idea I have in this whacky life. You're stuck with me, for better or for worse. <3

To my Kickstarter collaborators: Avery, Chris, Jerry, Jordan, Molly, Leda, Lauren, Roberto, and Justin—thank you for being a part of the first version of this project. Even if it didn't come to fruition in the way I originally thought it might, you believed in me and it and without you it wouldn't be what it is.

To my friends, my chosen family, and the powerful women in my life.

**Adriana** for promenading with me, sharing life with me, making me laugh harder than anyone I know, and for being my absolute ride-or-die, platonic soul mate. I love you, bitch.

**Leda** for our fireship and your sudden and kind encouragements that
have brought me to (happy) tears on more than one occasion (I screenshot them to read on sad days).

**Sausha and Annie** for the coffee shop days, holding my secrets, crying with me, and championing me in everything I do—the star and moon to my sun.

**Jordan** for sitting on FaceTime with me for literal days at a time, keeping it real, and doing all the ~*CrAzY*~ things with me.

**Diana** for reading and commenting on every post I make, opening your heart and home to me, and loving me no matter what.

**Jerry** for your kindness, patience, friendship through some of the hardest months of my life, and for your beautiful voice on the *other* audiobook version.

**Daniel and Shel** for your kindness, generosity, support, and for welcoming me into your family and creative orbit,

and to **Jonathan** for being the earliest reader of my words.

## *kickstarter supporters*

Adriana Castro, Aidan Mickle, Alex Burwell, Alicia Rials, Alyssa Buck Loughlen, Amanda Fetterly, Amanda OConnor, Andi, Andrea, Andrew Farnham, Andrew Watson, Andy, Andy Smith, Annie Ashley, Ashley Pae, Ava Strough, Barbara, Ben Harthun, Bill Carlson, Brent Jordan, Brian Merrel, Brittany, Christine Spencer, Christy Carlson Romano, Cierra Gibson, CJ Johnson, Claire Koleske, Clara Nguyen, Colleen Michal, Dan and Cait, Dan Laparra, David Fleming, David Walsen, David Wimett, Deane Miner, Elena Nola, Emily Levandowski, Emma Simon, Emmalie Kipp, Eva Gregory, Francisco Serrano, G, Gabi Duncombe, Gavin Verhey, George Winterin, HP, Jacqueline Castillo, jaeCHAOS, James Ihezue, Jill Eckhart, joe, John Riney III, John, Alberta, and John Arlo, Jordan Dené, Josh Lehenbauer, Kath Nash, Katie Bergl, Katie Jones, Kay Roth, Kendon and Melissa Shaw, Kevin Jeyakumar, Kimmi, Laura Hoerner, Lauren Dees-Pedroza, Leda and Taylor Costa van Putten, Lilith Rose, Lisa, Lisa Tim, Margaret, Maria Dyer-Santos, Marisa Younker, Matt Francisco, Matt Zeller, The McConvilles, Megan de Haan, Megan Marsden, Michelle Kucera-Jewell, Molly, Nancy Lara, Natalia, Nick Junke, Nick Miller, Nick Randio, Rachel, Rachel Motley, Rason Irvin, Raven Zoë, Rebecca Ann Decker, Rick Mann, Roberto Hoyos, Rose Adams, Rose Del Vecchio, The Ryans, Sarah Brooks, Sarah Goldschadt, Sarah Nicole Landry (@thebirdspapaya), Sausha Knott, Shannon Monroe, Sophia, Tara Theoharis, Tarah Peltz, Tash Haynes, Tim Johnston, Tom DeKeyser, Vic Chen, Vince Arminio, Zhora, and The Creative Fund by BackerKit

lead with love,
   chase laughter with sunshine,
   and always try to choose joy.
                xoxo, mal

www.ingramcontent.com/pod-product-compliance
Lightning Source LLC
Chambersburg PA
CBHW070350130626
46556CB00007B/3113